A Gift For:

_____

From:

_____

How to Use Your Interactive Storybook & Story Buddy:

1. Press your Story Buddy's ear to start.
2. Read the story aloud in a quiet place. Speak in a clear
   voice when you see the highlighted phrases.
3. Listen to your Story Buddy respond with several different
   phrases throughout the book.

Clarity and speed of reading affect Abigail's response.
She may not always respond to young children.

Watch for even more Interactive Storybooks and
Story Buddies. For more information, visit us on the
Web at www.Hallmark.com/StoryBuddy.

Copyright © 2011 Hallmark Licensing, Inc.

Published by Hallmark Gift Books,
a division of Hallmark Cards, Inc.,
Kansas City, MO 64141
Visit us on the Web at www.Hallmark.com.

All rights reserved. No part of this publication may be
reproduced, transmitted, or stored in any form or by any
means without the prior written permission of the publisher.

Editors: Emily Osborn and Megan Langford
Art Director: Kevin Swanson
Designer: Mary Eakin
Production Artist: Dan Horton

ISBN: : 978-1-59530-358-5
KOB8022
Printed and bound in China
APR11

BOOK 1

ABIGAIL
AND
The Balance Beam

By Lisa Riggin

Hallmark
GIFT BOOKS

Illustrated by
Lynda Calvert-Weyant

If ever there was a little girl who couldn't wait to grow up, it was Abigail. Every night before she went to sleep, she'd mark another day off the calendar. Every morning, she'd check to see if she'd grown taller.

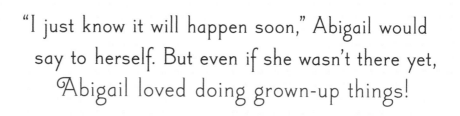

"I just know it will happen soon," Abigail would
say to herself. But even if she wasn't there yet,
Abigail loved doing grown-up things!

One of Abigail's favorite activities was gymnastics. She loved the costumes and the competition. Abigail would practice over and over to get every step perfect.

Today was the last practice before the final meet of the season, and Abigail worked as hard as she could. As she practiced, Abigail could hear her mom calling from the stands, "Abigail, you're doing a great job!"

Some days, though, things didn't go quite the way she wanted them to. Abigail whisked through all of her routines, but when she got to the balance beam, she fell off every time.

First, she weaved. Then she wobbled. Try as she might, she just couldn't make it to the end. Abigail wondered if she could ever do it.

Abigail was very quiet leaving the arena. She was thinking hard about her balance beam routine. "I'm so proud of you, Abigail," her mom said. "You're going to have so much fun on Saturday!"

Thinking about fun made Abigail smile.
Abigail always felt better after talking with her mom.

Finally, the big day arrived. Abigail put on the pink leotard her mom had made just for this day. Looking in the mirror, Abigail thought she looked just like the gymnasts on TV.

She practiced putting one foot in front of the other like she needed to do on the balance beam. "I can do this!" she thought. Abigail was very, very excited.

At the arena, the whole place buzzed with anticipation.
The people in the stands waved and clapped as the
gymnasts warmed up before the meet.

Abigail could barely contain her excitement as she stretched. "This is so grown-up," Abigail thought and smiled. Abigail loved doing grown-up things!

As Abigail hopped onto the trampoline for her first event,
she couldn't help worrying about her balance beam routine.
She was thinking about it even as she bounced and twirled
and dared to do the Hungarian Belly Flop – twice!

"An unusual move," said the judges. "And we like it!"

Abigail couldn't help but smile.

When it was time for the floor routine, Abigail really put on a show. No one else had thought to use hip-hop as a music choice.

Abigail almost forgot about the balance beam when her Slip and Slide and Popping and Locking brought the crowd to its feet. She could hear people yelling, "Abigail, you're doing a great job!"

Next, Abigail twirled on the uneven bars. She flew
through her routine. It was amazing to see Abigail hook
her little feet around the bar and spin one more time
before a perfect dismount.

The crowd went wild. But now Abigail was thinking
so hard about the balance beam she barely noticed.
She couldn't stop thinking about falling off.
Abigail wondered if she could ever do it.

She jumped onto the narrow beam and balanced.
One step, one jump, one handstand – and then it
happened. She wobbled!

But this time, she didn't fall. She made it all the
way to the end and stuck her landing.

Abigail's teammates gave her a high five.
Coach patted her on the back and said,
"Abigail, you're doing a great job!"

Abigail sat with her mom and waited for the awards ceremony. "I'm so proud of you, Abigail," said her mom. "But I wobbled," worried Abigail. "I bet if I were older, it would have been perfect."

"Being grown-up isn't about doing things perfectly," said Abigail's mom. "It's about doing the best you can, and that's exactly what you did." Abigail smiled. Abigail always felt better after talking with her mom.

"May I have your attention, please," blared the announcer over the loudspeaker. "The award for most points earned across all events goes to Abigail. Abigail, please come forward now to accept your prize."

Abigail won the biggest prize of all!

Abigail hugged her mom and then ran to the podium. This was the most exciting day of her life, and she wasn't even grown-up yet!

As the judge placed the medal around her neck, Abigail beamed with delight!

Did you have fun reading with Abigail?
We would love to hear from you!

Please send your comments to:

Hallmark Book Feedback

P.O. Box 419034

Mail Drop 215

Kansas City, MO 64141

Or e-mail us at:

booknotes@hallmark.com